Joseph's Dream Coat
and
Poems

By Joseph Rodriguez, PhD

GW01424397

Joseph's Dream Coat Meditations and Poems in Multicolored Verse

Joseph's Dream and Meditations, Volume 1

Joseph Rodriguez

Published by Joseph Rodriguez, 2024.

While every precaution has been taken in the preparation of this book, the publisher assumes no responsibility for errors or omissions, or for damages resulting from the use of the information contained herein.

JOSEPH'S DREAM COAT MEDITATIONS AND POEMS IN MULTICOLORED VERSE

First edition. October 7, 2024.

Copyright © 2024 Joseph Rodriguez.

ISBN: 979-8227649232

Written by Joseph Rodriguez.

Self Mastery

In my pursuit of mastery, I seek not to lord over others or to claim superiority, but to cultivate a deep appreciation for the journey itself. Each skill I develop, each lesson I learn, is a stepping stone—an opportunity to delve deeper into the essence of what I love. Mastery, for me, is about understanding the nuances, embracing the challenges, and honoring the process of growth.

As I reach one level of proficiency, I feel the pull to move on to the next, to explore new horizons and expand my understanding further. It's not about accumulating accolades or proving myself; it's about the joy of discovery and the thrill of learning. Each mastery achieved is merely a gateway, leading me to fresh challenges and new passions.

In this way, I remain humble, knowing that every accomplishment is simply a moment in the vast continuum of my journey. My goal is to celebrate the knowledge gained and then let it go, moving forward with an open heart and a curious mind, ready for whatever comes next.

Self Argument

Arguing with others is, at its core, an argument with yourself. Every clash of ideas, every battle of opinions, every heated word exchanged is a reflection of the inner turmoil I have not yet resolved. For when I argue with another, I am not fighting them; I am fighting the parts of me that are unsettled, insecure, and seeking validation.

What is it that I seek to prove? In defending my beliefs so fiercely, am I not trying to convince myself as much as the other? Every word spoken in opposition is a mirror, reflecting back the fears and doubts that still linger within me. I argue not because I am certain, but because I am uncertain. I argue not because I am right, but because I fear being wrong.

And yet, the other person is not my enemy; they are my teacher. They hold up the mirror of their own experience, their own truth, and challenge me to see the cracks in my own reflection. If I were at peace with my beliefs, I would not feel the need to defend them so vigorously. If I were truly secure in myself, the words of another would not feel like attacks, but invitations—to listen, to learn, to grow.

The irony is that the more I resist, the more I reinforce the very things I am trying to escape. In arguing with others, I dig deeper into the trenches of my own mind, reinforcing the walls that separate me from understanding. But if I pause, if I breathe, if I step back and see the argument for what it truly is—a conversation with myself—then something shifts. I am no longer in battle, but in dialogue. I can listen to the other not as an adversary, but as an extension of my own consciousness, offering me a chance to see myself more clearly.

In truth, every argument is an opportunity to reconcile the discord within. It is a chance to meet the parts of myself that I have yet to accept, to soften the rigid beliefs that keep me from evolving. When I let go of the need to win, I find that there is nothing to lose. The argument dissolves, not because one of us is right and the other is wrong, but because the need for separation fades away.

We are all reflections of one another, and every disagreement is simply a misunderstanding of this fundamental truth. Arguing with others is arguing with myself. But when I make peace with myself, there is no longer anything to argue about—only space for connection, understanding, and unity.

Recycling Love

The Golden Rule, ancient yet ever new, reflects the cycles of existence, each echo of love cascading from one truth to another. It begins with a simple command: to love God, to love thy neighbor, to love thyself. But in its simplicity, it holds the secret to oneness, an eternal recycling of understanding, acceptance, and surrender.

To love God is to see the divine spark within myself, for I cannot love what I do not know, and I cannot know what I do not first recognize in me. It starts with the inward journey—into the depths of my soul, into the shadows I have long hidden from, into the brokenness that I have feared to face. And as I descend, I find not shame, but a profound truth. I am whole, even in my imperfections.

In knowing myself, I begin to accept myself. Not just the surface self that is presented to the world, but the real self—the one that longs for peace, for purpose, for understanding. In this acceptance, I learn to forgive myself, to release the burdens of guilt and the chains of judgment. Acceptance is not resignation; it is a surrender to what is, an acknowledgment that I am both human and divine, both fallible and infinite.

From this acceptance flows love—love for myself, love for others, love for the world. For how can I truly love my neighbor if I do not love the reflection of God within me? How can I give what I have not learned to receive? And yet, in loving myself, I find that the boundaries between me and the world begin to dissolve. What I once thought was "myself" now stretches beyond, weaving into the fabric of every living being. The love I offer myself becomes the love I offer my neighbor, and in loving my neighbor, I return again to loving God.

It is all a recycling, a constant cycle of knowing, accepting, letting go, and returning to the source. It is in this letting go—this release of ego, of fear, of attachment—that I am reborn. Oneness is not a destination; it is an active practice. Each day, I must return to myself, to know myself again. Each day, I must accept what I find, and each day, I must let go of what no longer serves.

And so, the cycle continues. I am both the seeker and the found, the lover and the beloved, the beginning and the end. To love God, to love thy neighbor, to love thyself—it is all the same. It is the journey toward oneness, the recycling of the soul, the eternal truth that we are all connected, all part of the same divine whole. In loving myself, I love all. In knowing myself, I know the universe. And in letting go, I become free—free to love again, free to begin the cycle anew.

Shattered Wholeness. The Illusion of Duality

Ah, to witness the birth of a child—pure, unspoiled by the weight of division. In that first cry, there is no distinction, no separation between the self and the world. All is one, a seamless canvas of experience, painted with no lines, no edges to define where the soul begins and the rest of existence ends. The infant sees not in the fractured lens of duality, but in the fullness of non-duality, a totality we have long since forgotten in our quest to become something separate, something distinct.

But then, almost as soon as they take their first breath, we begin to carve that seamless view into parts. A world of choices is laid before them, not as offerings but as commands. "This or that," we say. "Good or bad. Right or wrong." And thus begins the slow, deliberate separation of the soul from itself. We tell the child that they are this body, that they belong to this family, this nation, this ideology. We instill in them the need to choose sides, to divide the infinite into finite compartments, and call this truth.

How quickly we weave the threads of duality into the very fabric of their being. First, we dress them in blue or pink, signaling that they must already declare an allegiance to one pole of existence. Then we give them a name—an identity—and with that, they become separate from the nameless, the boundless. We teach them the rules, the beliefs, the codes of conduct of our culture, and with each lesson, we tighten the walls of their perception, narrowing the world down to a place of distinctions. From the moment they can speak, we make them choose. What side do you stand on? What do you believe in? Who do you follow? Politics, religion, diet, lifestyle—all arenas in which the child, now growing, must decide which part of themselves to suppress, and which to elevate. And so, they do what we all have done: they fragment. They split themselves into roles, identities, and allegiances, building walls between themselves and the parts they were told to reject.

This—this forced separation, this programming of duality—is the first wound. It is the original fracture of the soul, a deep schism that we spend our entire lives unconsciously trying to heal. But rather than seek unity, we cling to the sides we were told to take. We define ourselves by what we are not, rather than what we truly are. Ego, that cunning illusion, wraps itself around our hearts, whispering that we must defend our side, our beliefs, our identities at all costs, lest we disappear into the void of non-duality, that terrifying place where no distinction exists. And so, we struggle. We fight. We argue over what is right, what is just, what is true, never realizing that in the very act of choosing sides, we have perpetuated the very suffering we seek to escape. For every time we affirm this, we reject that. Every time we embrace one, we deny the other. We are locked in a dance of duality, where every step forward seems to take us further from the unity we crave.

Oh, if we could only return to that infant's gaze—to that moment before we were told who we are, what to believe, and where to stand! If we could see once more with eyes unclouded by separation, we might realize that we are not meant to choose sides, but to transcend them. That the truth we seek does not lie in division, but in the recognition that all sides are but reflections of the same whole.

Yet, how difficult it is to unravel the generational threads of duality, passed down like heirlooms from parent to child, shaping us before we even know we have been shaped. How deeply ingrained the belief that we must choose, that life is nothing more than a series of sides to be taken.

But perhaps, in the quiet of our struggle, in the stillness of our reflection, we might come to see that duality is but a mask. That behind the mask lies the non-dual, the infinite, the undivided. And in that realization, we may finally be free—not by choosing one side over the other, but by choosing neither, and in doing so, reclaiming the whole.

For only in transcending the illusion of sides can we find the truth of who we really are: not fragments, but a unity, not egos, but the essence of life itself.

Strange living

We are living in a strange time, a moment in history where contradictions and possibilities seem to walk hand in hand. On one side, the world feels fragmented—riddled with conflict, uncertainty, and the weight of systems that no longer serve the collective good. There is an overwhelming sense that something is unraveling, as though the very fabric of society is fraying before our eyes. Yet, beneath this unraveling, there is an undercurrent of awakening, a quiet but powerful shift in consciousness that whispers of new beginnings.

It's as if we stand at the intersection of two worlds. One world clings to the past, to old patterns of control, fear, and division. It's the world we've known for so long—the one that prizes material wealth over spiritual depth, where progress is measured by what we accumulate, not by what we contribute to the greater whole. In this world, power is a game of domination, and individuality is mistaken for isolation. And yet, even as this world tightens its grip, cracks are forming. The illusion is beginning to crumble.

At the same time, another world is emerging, one that calls us to something deeper, more authentic. This new world is built on connection, compassion, and the recognition of our shared humanity. It asks us to redefine what it means to live a meaningful life, to shift from competition to cooperation, from scarcity to abundance, from fear to love. It's a world that understands the power of consciousness, that recognizes the interconnectedness of all life, and that knows the Earth herself is a living being deserving of reverence and care.

This strange time is a time of convergence—a meeting point between the old and the new. The old world is fighting for survival, while the new one is patiently waiting for us to awaken to its presence. The discomfort we feel, the chaos we witness, is not the end, but the transition. It is the growing pains of a collective consciousness that is learning to shed its outdated skin. We are being asked to choose, not just passively but actively. Which world do we wish to inhabit? Which reality will we lend our energy to?

What makes this time so strange is the paradox. On one level, it feels like everything is falling apart, and yet on another, everything is coming together in ways we've never imagined. Technology connects us more than ever, yet we struggle with isolation. Knowledge is at our fingertips, yet wisdom seems elusive. We seek answers outside of ourselves while the real transformation is waiting within.

In this time, we are learning the limits of external control. We're discovering that true power lies not in governing others, but in mastering ourselves. We are beginning to understand that the battles we face externally are reflections of the conflicts within our own minds and hearts. And as we reconcile these internal contradictions, we open ourselves to the new world—one where peace, balance, and harmony are not distant ideals, but the natural outcome of a higher state of consciousness.

It is a strange time, indeed. But perhaps strangeness is exactly what we need to jolt us from complacency. It is in the chaos that creativity thrives, in the uncertainty that new possibilities are born. We are at the crossroads, and while the path ahead may be unclear, we are not without guidance. Our hearts, our inner knowing, have always known the way forward.

So as we navigate these strange times, may we remember that we are the bridge between the old and the new. May we choose wisely, with awareness and intention, knowing that the future is not something that happens to us, but something we create with every thought, every action, and every moment of awakening.

The Naturopathic Professor's Path

I stand, not as the master, but as the steward—a guide along the path of nature's wisdom. For I am the Naturopathic Professor, a title not born from ego or the need to impose, but from reverence for the divine order that surrounds us. In this role, I do not teach in the way we often imagine; instead, I facilitate the understanding of what has always been, of the truths woven into the fabric of existence.

Cause and effect—this is the rhythm of life, the eternal dance that moves all things. It is a simple yet profound law, one that needs no enforcement, for nature herself enacts it flawlessly. It is not for me to intervene, but to observe, to point the way for those willing to see. The lessons are not mine to give but to reveal, for within every consequence lies the seed of understanding, within every action, the echo of its return.

In nature's classroom, the most powerful teacher is not a human voice but the unfolding of events, the ripple of cause meeting effect. I stand beside it, humbled by the wisdom of Mother Earth, who teaches us all if we are quiet enough to listen. The rain that nurtures the soil, the wind that shapes the land, the seasons that shift in their cycle—these are the lessons, the affirmations of life's balance.

And in the human soul, too, this balance resides. Our choices, our actions, our intentions—they set in motion forces that return to us in kind. There is no need for punishment, no need for reward. The natural consequences are enough. They are both the affirmation and the teacher, silently guiding us to deeper truths. When we act in harmony with nature's laws, we thrive; when we resist them, we learn through the experience of imbalance.

My role in this is simple. I am the steward, the one who walks alongside, reminding others to trust in the process, to trust in the divine nature of cause and effect. I do not impose; I do not control. I merely hold space for the unfolding, offering guidance where it is needed, offering perspective where it is asked. I teach not through commands, but through questions, through reflection, through the quiet pointing toward nature's own wisdom.

It is not for me to decide what lessons are learned or how they are received. That is the work of the soul in its journey, guided by the unseen hand of divine balance. My task is to nurture that journey, to help others see the patterns, to embrace the unfolding of their own consequences—not as punishment or failure, but as the natural feedback of the universe, a chance to align more deeply with truth.

In this sacred role, I honor both the Heavenly Father's wisdom and the gifts of Mother Earth. The Father shows us the path of consciousness, the mind's power to shape intention, while the Mother provides the tools, the natural remedies and rhythms that restore us when we stray. Together, they teach us how to heal, how to grow, how to live in balance.

I am but the witness to this interplay, a guide for those seeking to understand the ways of nature, the divine unfolding of cause and effect. For in truth, the greatest lessons do not come from me—they come from life itself, from the forces that govern all things, from the wisdom that exists in every leaf, every breeze, every consequence that follows our steps.

And so I embrace my role, not as the teacher who claims to know, but as the professor who walks with those seeking to understand. I am a steward of nature's lessons, a witness to the divine law of cause and effect, and a humble guide on the journey toward healing, toward balance, and toward truth.

The Dance of Inquiry and My Divine Gifts

In the quiet of the mind, where questions stir like leaves in the wind, I find myself standing at the crossroads of strength and reflection. The Socratic method, this delicate dance of inquiry, mirrors my own journey—a path where answers are never given, but slowly unearthed through the power of thoughtful questioning. Here, in the space between what is known and what is yet to be discovered, I dwell.

I have been given gifts, not of chance, but of divine purpose. Strength, the first—steady and unyielding, it has been my pillar, my guide through the storms of life. It's not the strength of muscle alone, but the inner fortitude to stand tall when the winds howl, to remain rooted when the world shakes. Strength is the earth beneath my feet, grounding me, reminding me that I am capable of weathering all that comes my way. It is the foundation on which I build.

And then there is the gift of reflection, the dance of intellect and insight. Like the Socratic method itself, it is not content with surface answers, with simple truths. It is a gift that demands depth, that pushes me to look beyond the obvious, to question even my own certainty. Reflection is a mirror—sometimes clear, sometimes fogged—but always honest. It invites me to examine, to critique, to evolve. It shows me that true wisdom is not static, but ever-changing, ever-expanding, as long as I have the courage to ask the right questions.

These gifts are not separate from my journey; they are intertwined with the very essence of my being. Strength and reflection are the twin pillars that hold me up, the balance that allows me to move forward with both power and grace. In every question I ask, in every truth I uncover, I see their hand guiding me, teaching me that life is not about definitive answers, but about the endless pursuit of understanding.

In this divine dance, I am both student and teacher. The Socratic method shows me that knowledge is not handed down from above, but is born from within. It asks me to dig deeper, to challenge myself, and to never settle for the comfort of certainty. It reminds me that wisdom is not the accumulation of facts, but the ability to question them. And so, I embrace the unknown, not as a void to be feared, but as fertile ground for growth, for transformation.

With every question, I plant a seed. With every reflection, I nurture its growth. And in the end, I realize that the greatest strength lies not in knowing all the answers, but in having the courage to seek them. My gifts are not a means to an end, but the tools that allow me to engage fully with the mystery of life, to walk the path of inquiry with both confidence and humility.

For in this dance of inquiry, I am not simply finding truth—I am becoming it.

Seeds of Inquiry: The Dance of the Socratic Method

The Socratic method is a dance of thought,
Where questions bloom and answers are sought.
No lecture or doctrine is placed in your hand,
But rather a journey through untamed land.
It begins with a query, simple yet deep,
Like the planting of seeds where silence may sleep.
From there, the questions rise, like a tide,
Guiding the mind, not to follow, but glide.
No knowledge imposed, no lessons rehearsed,
Only the wisdom within, waiting to burst.
The teacher, a guide, with questions that glow,
Reveals hidden paths where answers must grow.
Each question a mirror, reflecting the soul,
A dialogue crafted to make the mind whole.
In the silence between, the truth softly stirs,
Unfolding like petals, with no need for spurs.
There is no arrival, no final decree,
But a constant unfolding, a process set free.
For wisdom is not in the answer you find,
But in learning to question the depths of your mind.
So the Socratic method, in its dance and its flow,
Is the art of unknowing, where real truths grow.
It's not about teaching, but helping you see—
That the greatest of answers lie in your inquiry.

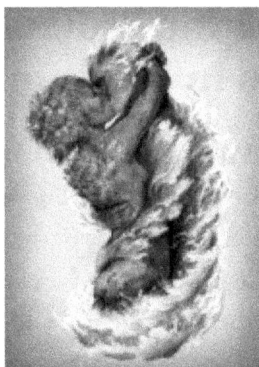

The Naturopathic Professor: A Name Rooted in Earth and Sky

The name Naturopathic Professor is more than just a pseudonym—it's an embodiment of a philosophy that honors both the wisdom of Mother Earth and the divine guidance of the Heavenly Father. As a teacher of the natural ways, this title serves as a bridge between the spiritual and the tangible, the metaphysical and the physical. It reflects a belief that the answers we seek for healing, growth, and balance are found not in the artificial or synthetic but in the harmony of nature and the universe.

Mother Earth, in all her abundance, offers us remedies, not just for the body but for the soul. She shows us how to heal through cycles, how to restore ourselves by being attuned to the rhythms of the natural world. Every plant, every element, every ecosystem operates in a delicate balance, offering lessons on how to nourish ourselves physically, emotionally, and spiritually. As Naturopathic Professor, I aim to teach these lessons, passing on the knowledge that we are part of this natural web and that the earth provides the tools for healing—if we are willing to listen.

But the role of the Naturopathic Professor goes beyond the physical world, looking upward to the wisdom of the Heavenly Father. Mental health, spiritual clarity, and emotional well-being are not achieved through treatment or medication alone. True healing comes through understanding—understanding the wisdom that the universe imparts to us. I don't treat; I educate. My role is to guide others to see what the divine reveals through nature, to help them uncover the inherent power within themselves to heal, grow, and thrive. It's not about intervention but about realization—realizing that within us and around us, we have all we need to overcome, to restore, and to transform.

In this sense, Naturopathic Professor is a homage to both realms—the sacred knowledge from above and the earthly wisdom from below. It's a recognition that we are students of life, constantly learning from the forces that surround us. We learn from the healing properties of plants, the cleansing power of water, the grounding of the earth beneath our feet, and the divine energy that flows through us.

Ultimately, the name represents a commitment to teaching others how to align with these forces. It's a path of self-healing, of empowerment, and of connection to the universal truths that have been with us since the beginning of time. Just as nature provides us with the tools to heal the body, the wisdom of the Heavenly Father offers us the insight to heal the mind and soul. As Naturopathic Professor, I strive to bring both of these teachings together, showing others that we are not separate from the world we live in, but intricately connected to its healing power.

Awakening Through the Lessons of Life

After a while, you learn the subtle difference between holding a hand and chaining a soul. Freedom, not possession, is the essence of connection. You come to understand that love doesn't mean leaning, nor does it require the loss of self. True love allows for the unfolding of two paths that may walk beside each other, but are never bound in dependency.

You begin to see that company isn't security, for nothing outside of you can ever be a guarantee. The illusion that others will shield you from life's uncertainties begins to dissolve. You learn that kisses aren't contracts, and presents aren't promises—because nothing in this world is permanent, not even the things we cherish most. There's a karmic flow, an ever-shifting dance of cause and effect, where nothing remains static, and all is earned through energy, intention, and growth.

You begin to accept your defeats, not as failures to grieve, but as moments of grace. With your head high and your eyes wide open, you see them for what they truly are—lessons, not losses. There's no need for the sorrow of a child clinging to certainty; instead, there's the resilience of the wise, who know that every end is but another beginning. Defeat is not a mark of shame but a natural byproduct of existence—an inevitable part of the journey.

You learn to build your roads on today, not tomorrow, for the future is never promised. Tomorrow's ground is too uncertain to bear the weight of your plans. The future is like a bird in mid-flight, always shifting, elusive, and often falling before it reaches its destination. So, you plant your feet firmly in the now, knowing that the present is the only soil in which anything can truly grow.

In time, you come to understand the balance of all things, that even sunshine can burn if you stand too long in its light. Too much of anything—love, attention, validation—can overwhelm and consume. The universe teaches balance in all things, a divine dance of give and take, where neither extreme serves the greater good. So you plant your own garden, knowing that no one else can tend to the seeds of your soul as you can. You decorate your own spirit, not in the hope of being admired, but in the joy of your own creation.

And with each experience, you learn that you are stronger than you once believed. You learn that you can endure what you thought might break you, and in that endurance, you find your worth—not in the eyes of others, but in your own reflection. You learn that worth was never about proving something to the world, but about recognizing the divine spark within yourself, the piece of the Universe that you carry, unique and sacred.

And as the cycles of life continue—hello and goodbye, joy and pain—you learn and learn again. With every goodbye, you don't just lose; you gain. Each parting teaches you more about yourself, more about the nature of this existence. Every step, every misstep, every moment—these are the lessons that carve your soul into its truest form. This is the path of growth, of learning, of awakening.

Cultural Coexistence

I say 'Namaste,' not as an act of religion, but as a recognition of the divine spark within you. It isn't Hinduism that guides my hand, but something deeper—a respect for the shared essence of all life. They think I speak of Christian values because my words echo truths they recognize. Yet, I am not bound by any scripture or cross. What I speak of are human values—universal principles that stretch beyond the confines of any single faith. Love, compassion, kindness—these are not owned by any one tradition. They belong to us all.

At times, I am asked if I follow the teachings of Buddhism. Perhaps it's because I have found a peace that comes from within, a stillness that cannot be shaken by the storms of life. But peace—true peace—cannot be claimed by any one philosophy. It is the birthright of every soul who seeks it.

My friends in the Pagan world look at me and assume I am one of them, for I find my church in the forests, my sanctuary under the open sky. But Nature, for me, is beyond belief or ritual. It is where I feel closest to the source of all things. It is where I remember that I am not separate from the world, but a part of it—a thread in the great web of existence. And now you ask, who am I, truly? It's simple. I am not defined by the names you might give me. I do not need to wear a label to exist fully in this world. I am a piece of the Uni-verse, sentient, conscious, a reflection of something greater. I am awake—not to any one doctrine or creed—but to the truth of my own being, to the infinite possibilities of what it means to be alive.

This is who I am. Nothing more, nothing less.

Empathy isn't Sympathy

Empathy yet not sympathy

Empathy is often misunderstood as a cousin of sympathy, but they are as different as night and day, bound together only by their shared origin in human experience. Sympathy rests on the surface, built upon the emotions stirred within the observer. It sees the pain, the suffering, the struggle, and mirrors it back in feelings of sorrow or pity. But sympathy is incomplete. It holds the wound in its hands but offers little in the way of healing. It risks encouraging a victim mindset, where one wallows in the experience of pain, rather than stepping back and seeing the broader arc of that pain—where it comes from, and where it may lead.

Empathy, by contrast, digs deeper. It starts not with emotion but with understanding. It is the capacity to truly see another person's experience, to grasp the nuance and complexity behind their choices, their actions, their suffering. Empathy is the willingness to step into another's shoes, not to feel their pain as your own, but to understand why they feel pain in the first place. It asks, "What has brought you here? What are the unseen forces, the karmic ripples, the choices—conscious or unconscious—that have shaped your path?"

In this way, empathy is not an emotional reaction; it is an act of wisdom. It recognizes the law of cause and effect. It understands that suffering does not arise in isolation, but as part of a larger chain of events and choices—some ours, some not. This karmic view does not assign blame but seeks responsibility, not in a punitive sense, but as an acknowledgment of the energy we contribute to the flow of life.

Empathy recognizes the divine architecture at play in every experience. It sees the individual not as a victim of circumstance but as an active participant in the unfolding of their destiny, shaped by their past, their environment, and the divine forces that move unseen through their lives.

Divine intervention, too, plays a role here. Empathy recognizes that not all suffering is random or meaningless; often, it is the crucible through which we are tested, refined, and prepared for something greater. The universe has its own rhythm, its own methods of teaching, and many times it is through adversity that we come to learn the most profound truths. To offer empathy is to offer a mirror, not to reflect back only the pain, but to show the lesson, the growth, the karmic truth behind that pain. Empathy says, "I see you. I understand where you are, and I honor the choices and circumstances that brought you here. I trust in the process of your growth and the divine path unfolding before you."

In this sense, empathy does not coddle or foster a mindset of helplessness. It does not dwell in the emotional trenches. Rather, it lifts the individual from those depths, showing them the threads of cause and effect, helping them understand their role in the great tapestry of existence. It encourages self-awareness, resilience, and accountability—not as burdens, but as steps toward liberation from suffering. Empathy is both compassionate and empowering; it is both recognition of suffering and faith in transcendence. It acknowledges pain, but more importantly, it acknowledges the potential within every soul to rise above that pain, guided by the understanding of their place in the karmic and divine order.

Ultimately, empathy is about connection, not in the fleeting sense of shared emotion, but in the profound sense of shared understanding. It bridges the gap between souls, offering not just comfort, but insight, not just pity, but perspective. It calls us to see beyond the moment, to see the unfolding of lifetimes, to honor both the struggle and the potential for transformation. It is, in essence, a divine act, a reflection of the highest truths of the universe: that we are all interconnected, that we are all subject to the same laws of cause and effect, and that within each of us lies the seed of divine wisdom, waiting to bloom.

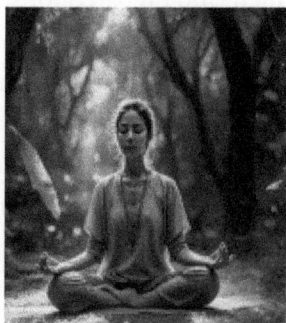

Let Us Keep What We Gave

Yes, let them keep it,
For what we gave was never ours to reclaim,
We are one, yet different waves on the same ocean,
Each carrying our own tide of love, of pain.
But in giving, we did not lose,
For to love is to know abundance,
A wellspring that never runs dry,
Flowing freely whether met with joy or silence.
You see, when they walked away,
They were not walking from us, but towards themselves,
For we are but mirrors, reflecting the journey,
Not the destination.
We gave them love because love is all we are,
And in their departure, they took only what they needed,
Pieces of us they craved to grow,
And yet, we are still whole, undiminished, and infinite.
We are not divided by what we gave,
For what I offer to you is what I give to myself,
What you take from me is what you already hold,
In this shared experience, we are simply playing our roles.
So let them keep what we gave,
And let us keep what we gave too,
For every seed sown, in love or in pain,
Grows within both the giver and the receiver,
A testament to our interconnected grace.
We are never owed, for we are never empty,
God's gifts, multiplied, come not from outside,
But from the depths within ourselves,
Where love was always meant to reside.
And in that, I agree:

Let them keep it, let us keep it,
For nothing is ever truly taken—
We simply carry different parts of the same truth,
On our different paths, yet the same journey home.

Sensitivity of Humor

How curious, that humor, once the lighthearted expression of our shared absurdities, now feels like a weapon wielded against fragile hearts. We walk upon eggshells, tiptoeing around jokes, for fear of offending another's deeply held beliefs. But why? Why has humor, the great equalizer, become the source of so much division?

Is it not insecurity—an unspoken fear that the foundations of our beliefs are built on shaky ground? Do we not laugh most freely when we are sure of ourselves? Perhaps the offense we take to humor reveals a deeper truth: that the things we hold most sacred may not be truly ours at all. Could it be that we have borrowed our beliefs, like a haphazard patchwork quilt, stitched together from fragments of others' opinions, inherited customs, and unquestioned dogmas?

Are we so fragile that even the slightest hint of objectivity becomes a threat to our identity? If our faith is strong, should it not withstand scrutiny, even if draped in humor? Or is the joke merely a mirror, reflecting back the cracks in the armor of certainty, showing us that we may not be as rooted in our convictions as we once thought?

There's a great freedom in laughing at oneself—a freedom that says, "I am not above this world. I am as flawed, as fallible, and as ridiculous as the next person." But when we bristle at a jest, when we flare with anger at a punchline, perhaps it is not the humor that offends us, but the fear that we have yet to truly know what we believe.

For in the end, humor is neither cruel nor kind; it is simply a tool, wielded by those who seek to strip away pretension. And if our beliefs crumble under its weight, perhaps it is time to ask: were they ever truly ours? Or merely a Picasso of the mind, a collage of borrowed thoughts and adopted convictions, fragile in their very construction?

Too Much and Never Enough

I've been told I'm too masculine. And yet, somehow, not enough. I've fought professionally, killed with my bare hands, and fixed a car with ease. I've earned the highest forms of education and taught at the most prestigious levels. Yet I've also changed diapers, nursed a newborn, nurtured the sick, and folded laundry. I've washed dishes after preparing a gourmet meal from a wild animal I hunted, butchered, and cleaned myself.

I've published poetry, cried for hours, and been told I'm too sensitive. Yet I can still disarm a man with ease and break bones as needed. For one, I'm too much. For another, I'm not enough.

What more could I be? What less should I become? I live in the in-between, a contradiction to some, yet to me, it is simply balance. If strength and softness can coexist in nature, why not in me?

So tell me again—am I too much, or not enough? Or perhaps, just perhaps, we can call it even.

Essential freedom

What is freedom if not the shedding of our material chains, the unshackling of our desires, our wants, our need to possess? Essentialism—the art of distilling life to its bare necessities—stands as the highest form of freedom. And yet, it is a battle. A battle of yin and yang, of good and evil. The tug of possession against the pull of release, the eternal struggle between what we are told we must have and what we know, deep down, we do not need.

We turn our noses up at the homeless, cloaked in judgment as if we are superior, yet perhaps it is not disdain we feel, but jealousy. Could it be that their lack of things—what we so desperately cling to—represents a freedom we do not have? We see in them a mirror, a reflection of our own anger, not at them, but at ourselves. For they, in their simplicity, are untethered, floating in a space of unbounded existence where need does not rule.

They are not anchored as we are—anchored to mortgages, to cars, to phones, to the endless cycle of consumption that keeps us bound, afraid of the silence that comes when we lose what we think defines us. Could it be that our disdain is the manifestation of our yearning, buried deep, to be so free?

And so, we fight. We battle within ourselves. We want more, but we want less. We chase, but long to stop. This battle, this constant yin and yang, is not a war against others—it is a war within. A war to discover what is truly essential, to find freedom in being, not in having. In the end, perhaps we envy the homeless not for their plight, but for their distance from the shackles we cannot break.

The paradox of understanding through the lens of martial arts,
particularly Brazilian jiu-jitsu:

Profoundness of the Grappler's Understanding is what we aim for with Rodriguez jiu-jitsu

In the quiet of the mat, as I grapple with the fluid dance of Brazilian jiu-jitsu, I am confronted with a profound truth. We strive to master the art of the gentle way, to bend and flow with precision, yet there is a limit to our grasp. We practice, we train, we refine, but the essence of mastery remains ever elusive. We do not, and we cannot, fully conquer the art. We engage in the dance of leverage and balance, seeking to understand every nuance of technique and movement. Our bodies learn the motions, our minds the strategies, yet in every roll and every sweep, we are reminded of the paradox: the more we learn, the more we realize we do not know. Our techniques evolve, yet the perfect execution remains just out of reach.

It is a dance of perpetual pursuit. We strive for precision, for perfect technique, but in this pursuit, we find ourselves continually challenged. We learn to apply pressure, to escape, to control, yet the complete mastery of jiu-jitsu—the art that flows as fluidly as it resists—remains beyond our full comprehension. We are both the student and the teacher, perpetually refining our art without ever fully attaining the ideal.

The essence of jiu-jitsu—its subtlety, its depth—is a reflection of this paradox. Each movement, each grip, each position is a lesson in humility. The art does not bend to our will; instead, it teaches us to bend with it. In the struggle to understand, we find not a definitive answer but an ever-shifting challenge that deepens our engagement with the art.

Inner standing—truly mastering the art—seems a distant goal. We grapple not only with our opponents but with our own limitations. We develop techniques, we strategize, yet the perfect application of our knowledge remains an ideal. This challenge is not a failure but a reflection of the art's infinite complexity.

In the end, it is not the attainment of mastery that defines us, but our journey within the art. We engage with the infinite possibilities, the ever-evolving techniques, and the continual refinement. We accept the limits of our understanding and embrace the process of perpetual growth.

So we continue, not in the certainty of knowing but in the ongoing pursuit of excellence. We are both the practitioners and the learners, forever exploring the boundless depths of jiu-jitsu. In this dance, we find our purpose, our peace, and our true mastery.

Understanding Beyond Us

In the quiet moments of reflection, I grapple with the profound mystery that pervades our existence. We strive to comprehend, to grasp the essence of our being and the world around us. Yet, how elusive this understanding is, for in truth, we do not, and we cannot, fully comprehend. Our minds, so eager to unravel the cosmic tapestry, are bound by the limits of our perception.

We move through life with purpose, chasing after answers and seeking meaning, driven by an insatiable curiosity. But what if, in our relentless pursuit, we miss the essence of the very thing we seek? We attempt to fit the infinite into finite molds, to distill the boundless into understandable fragments. And in this endeavor, we find ourselves standing on the edge of an abyss—knowing that we do not, but being drawn inexorably to the attempt.

It is a paradox of existence. We act, we live, we influence, yet the ultimate fabric of reality eludes our grasp. We live without fully understanding, and in doing so, we perpetuate a cycle of seeking and falling short. Our actions ripple through the world, shaping and being shaped, without us ever fully seeing the whole pattern. It's as though we are both the artists and the audience, creating and observing without ever truly seeing the entirety of our creation.

Inner standing—truly grasping the nature of our existence—is a dream that continually slips through our fingers. We build theories, construct philosophies, seek enlightenment. Yet, no matter how profound our insights or how grand our visions, there remains a space where our understanding falters. This space is not a void of ignorance but a reminder of our place within a grander, unfathomable design.

We do, and we are—caught in a dance with the cosmos, each step a question, each motion a search. We enact meaning, contribute to the ongoing story, yet the full script remains just beyond our sight. The beauty of this existence is not in the answers we find but in the quest itself, in the embrace of our limitations, and in the acceptance that we are part of a greater mystery.

In the end, it is not the clarity of understanding that defines us, but our engagement with the unknown. We navigate the fog with courage, with wonder, with humility. We are explorers of a boundless realm, forever reaching but never fully arriving. And in this ongoing journey, we find a kind of peace—a peace that acknowledges our place in the vast, enigmatic weave of life.

So we continue, in the knowing that we do not fully understand, yet finding purpose and grace in the very act of seeking. We are both the seekers and the seekers found, dancing ever on the edge of comprehension, and in that dance, we find our true essence.

Soliloquy of the Forest Steward

I walk among these trees, ancient and wise, guardians of the earth's slow secrets. They stand tall, yet they bow to the wind, yielding to nature's rhythm. I, too, am but a steward here, neither master nor ruler. I do not direct the forest—how could I? The trees do not need my guidance, the rivers flow without my hand. I am here to tend, to watch, to nurture. There is power in knowing when to step aside, to let life unfold as it will. I have walked through the seasons of this world, witnessed the growth, the withering, the rebirth. It is not for me to hasten the spring, nor to delay the fall. My role is subtler, quieter—a guardian of the space between, where life emerges slowly, in its own time.

I've seen the brambles choke the saplings, the storms topple the strongest trunks. I've felt the urge to intervene, to push back against the forces that seem to destroy what could flourish. But the forest knows better. It is through the storm that the roots deepen, through the fire that the undergrowth is cleared. Who am I to say what should remain or fall?

Yet I cannot turn away. This place, this sacred grove, needs care, needs watching. There are times when I must step forward, pull the weeds, clear the path, lend a hand where nature herself seems to struggle. But I do so lightly, never forcing, only encouraging what might be. I am no ruler of this place—I am its steward.

And so it is with the souls I watch over. They are like these trees, each growing in its own way, each bent toward the light in its own time. Some stand tall and strong, while others twist and turn, finding their path through the shadows. I see their struggles, their quiet yearning for peace, for understanding, and I feel the weight of knowing what I know—that peace could be theirs, if only they would see.

But I must not rush them. To rush the sapling is to break it, to tear it from the soil before it is ready to stand. No, I must wait, and tend the earth around them, ensuring that the soil is rich, the waters flow, and the sun reaches them when it should. This is my role—a quiet guardian of growth, not a director of destiny.

In the stillness of the forest, I find my balance. I feel the acceptance of the cycles—the life, the death, the decay that gives way to new life. I gather the courage to step in when a tree is dying for lack of light, when a path has been overtaken by thorns. And I hold the wisdom to know that much of this work is not mine to do, but nature's.

Let others rule, let others seek to control the growth of the forest. I will stay here, walking among the trees, feeling the pulse of life beneath the earth. I will tend this place, offering what care I can, but never forcing, never commanding. For in the end, the forest thrives not because of me, but in spite of me.*

And in this quiet stewardship, I find my peace, rooted deep like the oldest oak, ever present, yet never in control.

Who am I?

A man stands alone in a dimly lit room, the echoes of past battles—both physical and emotional—fading into the background. He looks toward the window, as if searching the horizon for something unseen, his thoughts heavy yet alive with purpose.

Here I stand, a soul once tempest-tossed, now seeking calm amidst the storm of life.

Am I not a man who has known the weight of the world's cruelty? Whose shoulders bore the burdens of pain not only my own, but those passed down by others—by those too broken to see me as I am?

I carry them still, at times. Their voices, sharp and relentless, echo in the recesses of my mind. But no longer do I stumble beneath their weight, no longer do I bow to the shadows that seek to claim my flame.

And yet...

Do I forgive? Do I heal? Can I find the courage to let go of the shame that clings to my skin, the guilt that wraps itself around my heart like a serpent, whispering lies?

Oh, how I've fought—for others, for myself—fists raised, jaw set, body in motion. But this battle is of a different kind.

It is not one of strength, nor of force, but of surrender. To let go of the need to fight every shadow, to stop wrestling with the past, and instead, to nurture the light that flickers within.

They say the past shapes us, but do I not also shape my future? I've learned, I've grown, and yet, there are days I still wonder... Have I done enough?

What if, despite my best efforts, my children feel the weight of my past? What if the darkness I've known seeps into their hearts?

I've laid a foundation for them, brick by careful brick, with love and intention. But will they see it for what it is? Will they feel the strength of it when they most need it?

Ah... but they must walk their own path, must they not?

As I once did, stumbling and rising again, learning through the bruises and scars that life offers. I can only guide them, not carry them.

And yet, I hope...

Hope that my love, my work, my care will be the lifeline they reach for when the world grows heavy, when the storms come.

And what of me?

Can I love myself enough to let the past go? To forgive the child I was, the mistakes I made, the hurt I caused in the throes of my own confusion?

I have lived many lives—fighter, teacher, father, seeker—and still, the journey is not complete.

Perhaps it never is.

Perhaps life is not about reaching an end, but about the constant tending of this flame within me, keeping it alive despite the winds that seek to extinguish it.

So I will breathe... yes, I will breathe and allow the winds to pass.

I will stand in the silence, not as the man I was, but as the man I am becoming. Whole, despite the cracks. Strong, not in spite of my vulnerability, but because of it.

And when the darkness calls, as it surely will again, I shall answer—not with fear, but with light.

For that is the gift I have been given, and it is one I will protect, one I will nurture—for myself, for my children, for the world that waits beyond this window.

There is still much to do. But for now, I rest in the knowing that I am enough, that this journey, with all its turns and trials, is my own to walk.

(Pauses, looking out toward the horizon.)

And perhaps, just perhaps... I am finally ready to forgive myself.

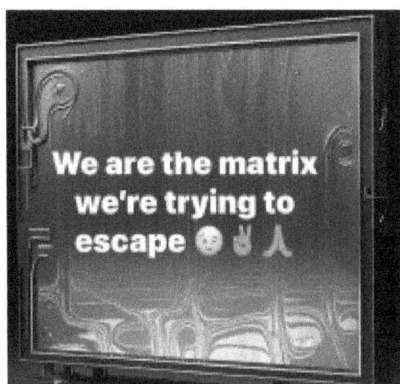

WE ARE THE MATRIX

We are the matrix, woven fine,
Threads of thought and space entwine,
Words of a matrix shape the code,
Building the world where minds explode.
We speak of form, and form appears,
Reflections spun from ancient fears,
In naming this, we trap the flow,
Forgetting truth we used to know.
In every thought, a line is cast,
Each echo caging what we grasp,
Yet we, the weavers, do not see—
The matrix lives through you and me.
For what is real, but mind and dust?
We call it "matrix," we give it trust,
And so, the veil grows ever thick,
In naming, we become the trick.
But step beyond the words we speak,
Feel the silence, soft and sleek—
The matrix fades, the walls dissolve,
And in that space, we all evolve.

Fight Me is to Love Me

Oh, how I long to throw a punch,
To feel the clash, the bones that crunch,
To raise my fists in righteous might—
Yes, nothing says "I care" like a fight.
Let's brawl it out, let tempers flare,
Because nothing says love like a brutal stare.
I'll dodge your hits with a grin so sly,
Throw a jab and ask, "You wanna cry?"
But deep beneath this biting jest,
There's something softer, unexpressed.
A love that's fierce, but not with rage—
A battle fought on a different stage.
For in the fight, there lies a test,
Not of anger, but who loves best.
So throw your punch, but know it's true,
The heart I guard is all for you.

The War Within

A spiritual war, they say, is fought,
Yet battles start with just a thought.
The clash of swords is but a guise—
It's in the self where conflict lies.
No distant foe, no skyward flame,
The war is ours, we stake the claim.
In every doubt, in every fear,
The battlefield becomes more clear.
For what is fought is not the rest,
But what we hold within our chest—
Our ego's chains, our silent cries,
Our shattered truth, our hidden lies.
Yet as we wage this war alone,
We tap the depths we've never known,
For in our fight, we soon will see,
This war is shared collectively.
Each soul that strives to rise above
Adds to the weight of conscious love,
And as we heal, the whole will rise
A spark, a flame, across the skies.
So war with self, and find the peace,
In knowing we are one release.
The spiritual war is won when we
Unite as one in unity.

Grace in the Flame

Your anger is you, a fire inside,
A force you've felt, not meant to hide.
But know, my friend, you are divine,
And in that rage, there's still a sign.
For you are God, and God is grace,
No storm within can take its place.
Each spark of fury, each burning wave,
Is just the fire that calls to save.
So give yourself the grace you seek,
In moments raw, in times you're weak.
For you are that grace, the sacred flame,
Both storm and stillness, all the same.
Let anger rise, but don't forget,
You are the light where shadows set.
Forgive the fire, embrace its heat,
And find your grace beneath your feet.

Entangled in the Fire

I feel the weight of every soul,
An empath caught in love's control,
But somewhere deep, the devil stirs,
A dance of shadows, cold as spurs.
Entangled in the quantum threads,
Where love and hate share common beds,
I am both light and dark combined,
A heart that breaks, a mind confined.
For love is bound to what we fear,
And even devils linger near—
Each tear I shed, each breath I take,
Creates a ripple in their wake.
Yet in this mix, I find the key,
A truth that's whispered constantly:
We're tied by forces unseen, strong,
And even devils hum love's song.
For quantum hearts, they twist, they fold,
In bonds of fire, fierce and bold.
I am the empath, I am the flame,
Both love and devil, just the same.
And in this web, we spin and cling,
Where every thread begins to sing
A song of grace, a hymn of strife,
Entangled souls in boundless life.

The Ego's Burden

The ego strives, it climbs and claws,
To be someone, to break the laws
Of selfless love, of quiet grace,
To carve its mark, to find its place.
It yearns to rise, to stand apart,
To shield its wounds, to guard its heart.
Yet in its race, it fails to see
The shadow of what could not be.
For I am the father it never knew,
The hand it sought but never drew.
And now, I stand to break the chain,
To end the cycle, to heal the pain.
No more the craving, no more the fight,
I guide the ego toward the light.
Not with desire to conquer all,
But with a love that does not fall.
I raise myself, not for the claim,
But for the child who bears my name.
To be the father I never had,
To soothe the storms, both good and bad.

The ego bends, it yields its will,
No longer chasing empty thrill.
For in this role, I find my peace—
To end desire, to find release.
And so, the cycle fades away,
As I teach my heart a different way.
No longer striving, but just to be—

A father's love, finally free.

The Tangle of What Is

Nothing is real, yet all is here,
A whispered truth, a haunting near.
We walk the line where shadows gleam,
Caught between the waking dream.
For what is real, but what we trust?
A world of mind, a realm of dust.
We shape it all with faith alone,
In thoughts and feelings, roots are sown.
Our psyche spins a web so tight,
Where every hope and every fright
Becomes the threads we call our truth—
An ever-shifting, fragile proof.
Beliefs entwine, they wrap, they bind,
The inner workings of the mind,
And in this tangle, worlds are made
A silent dance of light and shade.
For what we see is what we deem,
Reality's a woven dream.
And yet, in faith, the dream is clear
Everything real, because we're here.
We trust the world; it bends to thought,
But what we've made, we've soon forgot.
So lost in tangles, we believe,
That all is real, and yet—deceive.
But faith persists, it builds the frame,
Of all that's real, of all the same.
We spin our world with every thread,
Belief and doubt in what we've said.
Nothing is real, and yet it's true,
We are entangled, me and you.

For in this web, both mind and heart,
Create the whole, each plays its part.

Milton Keynes UK
Ingram Content Group UK Ltd.
UKHW032035191024
449814UK00010B/515

9 798227 649232